from Acts to Testimonies

A COLLECTION OF REAL-LIFE STORIES OF FAITH

BY ADRIAN READ

From Acts to Testimonies

Trilogy Christian Publishers

A Wholly Owned Subsidary of Trinity Broadcasting Network

2442 Michelle Drive, Tustin, CA 92780

For information, address Trilogy Christian Publishing

Rights Department, 2442 Michelle Drive, Tustin, CA 92780.

Trilogy Christian Publishing/ TBN and colophon are trademarks of Trinity Broadcasting Network.

For information about special discounts for bulk purchases, please contact Trilogy Christian Publishing.

10 9 8 7 6 5 4 3 2 1

Library of Congress Cataloging-in-Publication Data is available.

ISBN 979-8-89597-050-8

ISBN 979-8-89597-051-5 (ebook)

THIS BOOK IS DEDICATED TO:

all of the beautiful, strong, and unwavering
Prayer Warriors. You have been and continue
to be an inspiration. May your endless
testimonies glorify His Kingdom!

ACKNOWLEDGMENTS

Adrian Read would like to thank Warrior Nation Ministries (Dr. Kellie Agueze), The M633 Movement (Apostle Sino Agueze), Kelly K Ministries (Evangelist Kelly Kopp), The Trinity Broadcasting Network and Mount Calvary Missionary Baptist Church (Pastor Melvin Blocker and First Lady/Minister Linda Blocker) for their priceless teachings.

You each have changed and influenced lives far more than you will ever know. May God continue to increase and bless your lives and your ministries.

INTRODUCTION

The pain I feel is real. My circumstances are real. When I cry out, is anyone listening?

Is there a higher power, a spiritual being that hears all? Are my prayers being heard? Will my prayers be answered? Are miracles real? Do miracles exist?

I need a miracle now!

There are times in our lives when we question the existence of God. We wonder if the answer to our prayers will come in time.

This book is a compilation of true real-life testimonies from people that have lived and experienced them, some of which have been passed down, inspiring each generation that hears them. I pray that they do the same for you.

TABLE OF CONTENTS

Chapter 1

———⚭———

The Low Ground

There was a woman. She was not rich, nor did she have any money in the bank. What she was was a mom. A praying mom. An African American mom living in the 1940s. She had become a widow with many children. She owned one plot of land among many plots that were owned by others. The plot was a beautiful piece of land that sat up on a hill.

One source of income was to plant crops on that land to help make ends meet. Her family had done this for several years.

A day came when it was time to take the kids out of school to help her tend the field. It was time to get the field ready for the next crop.

They worked from sunup to sundown, and finally it was done. Until…there was a knock on the door.

This man…standing there. A person of authority. Another woman wanted this mom's land. This man came to say that the field that she and her kids just finished was now being turned over to this woman, the new owner, and that the new owner's field was now this mother's property. A swap. Her family had worked so hard on this field just to have it taken from them in an instant.

The mother pleaded and pleaded. It just fell on deaf ears. This was a fight she could not win. Or could she?

The mom wondered what condition the field was in that they were left with.

When she saw it, it was like starting from scratch. The field that sat low needed so much work. It meant keeping the kids out of school even longer. The mom cried. She prayed. She cried and prayed even more. Bottom line: no crop, no income. The mom and her kids started working in the new field.

Prayer was center stage with this mom. Pacing the floor and looking out the window up to where cometh her help.

Finally, it was done. The new field was done. There's only time, the time it takes to wait for harvest.

With harvest time approaching, more and more prayers went up.

One day, this mom looked out of the window she had looked out of countless times before with tears in her eyes and started humming. Not just any hum but one that felt like it was coming from somewhere deep. As if her soul was reverberating from her body. Moments later, dark clouds covered the sky bringing with it a tremendous rain. The rain fell and kept falling, so much so that water was sitting with no place to go.

Every field owner was worried about their crops. When the rains stopped, it was time to assess the damage. Could they salvage anything?

As she arrived, passing the very woman that had taken her land, people were staring. The murmurs. "Everything is ruined except for one field," they said. Her old field sat high. What was believed to be an ideal spot. The new field sat low. Surely her field didn't survive the rains.

As she looked out, a tear rolled down her face. How can this be? How can this one field, the new field that sits low only look as though it had been sprinkled with water? How could this field have no mud? This field, in the midst of many fields that are all covered in a blanket of water. Those crops...*ruined*. How can this one field have the most beautiful vegetables? As if they had been drawn and painted by God? Her crop. The *only* crop that survived the storm. *Those* vegetables went for top dollar.

Lesson to be learned:
Don't mess with a praying mom.

Chapter 2

———⚭———

One-Way Ticket

There was a woman living in what most would consider paradise. It was all that she wanted. An answer to her prayers. But it took a toll on her financially to make that dream a reality.

One day she received the news she had been waiting months to hear. Her granddaughter had been born. She was elated. All she could think about was holding this little girl in a male dominated family.

Her excitement soon turned to concern. She lived almost 5,000 miles away. Not only did she have plans on traveling, but her elderly mother also needed to kiss the cheeks of this new arrival. That would mean purchasing two roundtrip tickets. This was not going to be a cheap flight. Money was tight. Very tight. How was she going to accomplish this? She not only wanted to go, but she wanted to be able to do or buy whatever she wanted while she was visiting.

She thought to herself, "Why am I worried? I know who I serve." She walked back and forth in her living room proclaiming to God that, because she was His child, she was leaving it in His hands. She then made a bold decision. She told God that she was going to buy a one-way ticket for her and her mom, but HE would have to get them back home.

She reminded Him that, in His Word, He asks us to try Him. So she did. She purchased those one-way tickets just waiting to see what God would do.

The day came for the two of them to head to the airport. Still nothing. No unexpected check in the mail. Nothing! But she stood firm. The two of them headed to the airport.

Once they got to the terminal, they were exhausted. All the walking and fighting crowds, but finally they were in their seats waiting to board the plane.

Suddenly, there was an announcement overhead. Due to overbooking they were asking for volunteers to give up their seats in exchange for airline vouchers.

Allowing her flesh to take hold (what we ALL have a tendency to do) she called her son to tell him what was going on. "Does this seem right?" she wondered. Should she answer the call? Her son firmly said, "If you don't get out of your seat and go up to that counter, you're about to miss your blessing!"

She got up, but by this time, the line was long. She was nearly the last person in line. There was no way she was going to be selected with so many people ahead of her. She waited and finally got up to the counter. They took her and her mom's name and said that, if selected, they would call their names.

It seemed like forever for them to start boarding the plane. They began calling the first group to board. She began to hear names called overhead. Their names had not been called. Another group began boarding. She started recognizing people that were in line earlier, opting to give up their seats, now boarding the plane. They gave their names first. How could they be boarding the plane? Group after group boarded until she looked around to find that there were but a few left in the terminal. All of a sudden, she heard their names.

She walked up to the counter where the agent apologized for the wait and offered her a voucher for her and her mother to be used towards anything related to the airline, a night's stay in a hotel and transportation to and from the hotel. To her amazement, the amount of both tickets not only covered their flight back but also was enough to take another trip in the future.

Lesson to be learned:
Stepping out on faith has its rewards.

Chapter 3

―――――∞―――――

Weathering the Storm

There was a young mom. She had just given birth and was now home recuperating.

About a week had passed. She turned on the television to the news. There was a storm brewing in the Atlantic Ocean. A Category 1 storm. Where she lived, storms came and went all the time, and the News showed no cause for immediate concern.

When she was younger, she had dreamed of becoming a meteorologist. She loved studying the weather. There were countless times a storm would be on its way, and she would get out a map and try to track it, predict where it was going. This time was no different. She got out her trusty map and began doing what she had done so many times before. She grew up in this area and had seen storms time and time again, but this storm was different. She could see the eye of the storm get more defined. She had a bad feeling about this one, a feeling that she couldn't shake.

As the days went on, she noticed that the storm was headed right for her. It was now a Category 3 storm. What was she to do? The home she lived in was not in the best condition. There was even a window that did not fully close. She has no supplies, nor did she have enough money to go out and purchase them. She scrounged up all that she could and walked to the corner store for whatever food and supplies she could afford.

The storm updates were continuing to roll in. It was now a Category 4. It was due to make landfall that night. The people on the television were not bothered by the updates at all.

They were throwing hurricane parties, laughing and joking as if it were just another day.

As the weather worsened, she began to pray for those not recognizing the force of nature headed their way. She also prayed for her household and those that dwelled inside. She asked God to cover them and shield them from the storm. She continued to pray throughout the night.

Clang…bang were the noises she heard. The windows shuttered. That one window that worried her so looked as though it would give way to the storm at any minute. At one point, the noise was so intense that it sounded like two freight trains were going to collide at the corner of her house. The roof shook. She just knew that this was it. The roof was going to come off. In that moment, she heard a voice within her saying that she needed to open another window. So she ran to the opposite side of the house and cracked open that window. There's no explanation as to why, but immediately, the pressure within the house subsided. She peaked out of the window just in time to see a massive sheet of metal tumbling down the street as if it were a leaf in the wind. It was terrifying! For her, at least. She was relieved to see that despite all of the ruckus happening, the children slept through it all. Totally and utterly at peace.

The next morning, she thanked God for her answered prayer. She noticed that her house still had power. When she turned on the news, she learned that the hurricane had made landfall as a Category 5 storm. She stood frozen in place in awe of what she was witnessing. There was complete devastation just south of her location, right where the eye of the storm had traveled. She knew that God's hand was at work. Of all the storms she had tracked, this one was an eye opener. She was grateful. Her family and home had weathered the storm.

Lesson to be learned:
But by the grace of God…

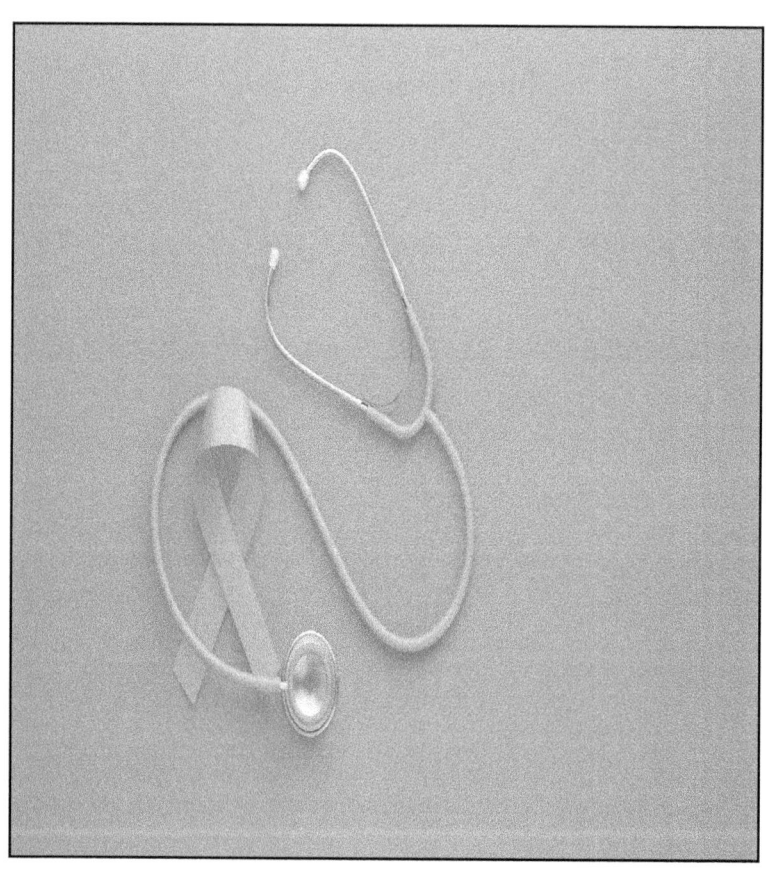

Chapter 4

The Scare

She had been relatively healthy her entire life. She had put on a few pounds as she got older, but who hadn't? One year, it was time for Open Enrollment for her insurance, and because she had reached a certain age, they recommended that she get a mammogram. Oh yes, the dreaded mammogram! I promise that if they did to men what happens to women during this process, it would be outlawed, and the powers that be would come up with a better way! But I digress. Needless to say, she made the appointment without thinking twice about it. When she went to her appointment. The office performed the mammogram, and she went about the rest of her day.

While at work, she got a phone call. She looked at the caller ID, and it was the doctor's office where she had her mammogram. So she answered. The woman on the other end was very pleasant. During the pleasantries, she stated that her mammogram came back with some irregularities, and that they would like to have her come back to the office. The woman said a lot of other stuff about what it all meant, but as soon as she stated irregularities and started to explain that they needed to do a biopsy, she didn't hear anything else. That moment became a fog of her existence. Was she trying to tell her that "the girls," as she frequently called her breasts, had turned on her? Suddenly, she was overcome by fear. So many thoughts went through her mind. Should she cry? Should she scream? Should she crawl up into the fetal position in the middle of her bed? What about her kids? What happens now? She then thought and reminded herself whose child she was and said, "God's got me!"

When she went to her follow-up appointment, they did another mammogram. The doctor stated that, in his words, "At least we are catching it in time." They then prepped her for the biopsy. During the biopsy, she just kept telling herself what God had promised: That as His child, sickness had no place in her body. That sickness had no home there. She then told God that she was turning her body over to Him.

After the procedure, she got dressed and walked out of there knowing, truly believing that God would keep His Word. You see, there were many things that led up to this moment. This display of faith. She had been reading the Bible, talking to others about His goodness, fasting throughout each and every month, praying and spending time with God throughout the day by either listening to praise music or listening to sermons and teachings. God's Word had become a part of her. It was her. So how could she be doing all of this and not trust in Him when it mattered?

She eventually got the results back. Negative for cancer. The words that so many long to hear.

Lesson to be learned:
Spend quality time with God and then...
STAND. ON. FAITH!

Chapter 5

---∞---

Faith Deposit

Home ownership is the desire of many people. This was no different for this young woman and her family.

She had made some poor financial choices in the past. She had prayed for a home, and for the longest time, she would try to improve her odds. She would save and do things to try to improve her credit. But every time she attempted something that the world told her she needed to do to qualify, something would happen. It's as if she was taking one step forward followed by two steps backward. After years of trying, she began to talk to God again about her situation.

She remembered that God had spoken to her and told her to "stop worrying about your credit. What you're doing won't matter." How could that be? Would someone be giving her a home? Would she be winning one? How else could you get a home with no money saved and bad credit?

She began affirming daily, "Lord, lead us to getting into our new home. I decree and declare that I will receive my home this year and the way that I receive it I will only have you to thank and others will have no choice but to acknowledge you." She did this each day for months. Eventually, a year passed. She began feeling discouraged. She said to God, "You said to test you, and that is what I am doing. You said in Your Word that as *YOUR child* all we have to do is ask, and so I'm asking." She began listing everything she wanted in a home. She prayed over the list and placed it in her prayer cloth. She then told God, "I'm turning it over to You." She began looking at houses online that were out of her price range, touring houses and walking through them as if she could write a check for whatever they asked.

One day, she received notification from a company on her phone that her credit score had increased. You see, the last time she checked, which was only a month ago, there were many recent negative items on it. She decided to humor herself by checking to see what her new report showed. Her eyes widened. She was speechless. Could this be? Was she looking wrong? This has got to be a mistake. She looked again to realize that every negative item on her credit report was gone! No collections. No late payments. No low score. Her credit score had not only increased but was now reporting as having good credit.

In the past, an item or two would be removed from her report just to see it return the very next month. She thought to herself that, when she checks next month, if it's still in good standing, she's going to get her house!

The very next month, still good! She decided to take a trip to the area in which she wanted to purchase a home and said to God, "When I come back, I'm going to have papers to my new home. All I ask is that while we are looking at houses, guide us. When we get to the one that YOU have for us, let them ask for this exact dollar amount." Off they went…

It was a Saturday morning; they toured one house, then another. Eventually, they were traveling down a road, and she was led to go into this new community. They got out of the car and walked inside of the model home. At each turn she liked the house more and more. It felt warm and familiar. It checked all the boxes on the list she had written to God of what she wanted in a house. The sales agent stated that they just began building the first fourteen houses. They asked if any that were being built were the same floor plan as the model? He stated that there was one being built further down the street. The community was still mostly land. Even so, as they walked to the property, she could see them living there. The house was just framework as they walked through it. She envisioned pulling in the driveway, sitting on the porch, cooking in the kitchen, and seeing a new bedroom set in the master bedroom.

Soon it was time to leave. The agent gave them a folder with different floor plan options, and they proceeded to go see other houses.

They had been driving for about thirty minutes, still talking about the house, when her phone rang. It was the agent. He stated that, if they liked the house, they could put down a good faith deposit. She asked the agent how much they would need? Wouldn't you know, the agent said the exact amount she told God. A smile came to her face. Without batting an eye, they turned their car around and headed back to what they knew was to be their new home.

When they returned, they talked with the agent who revealed to them that because it's a new community and with those being the first homes in the neighborhood, there were specials they could take advantage of. One was that they were offering money that could be used towards the down payment. For what the house cost, it was exactly the amount they needed.

They later walked through each section of the house praising God's name. They began writing scripture on the frames of each room. Amazed at God's work.

Months passed. Obstacle after obstacle. Delay after delay. She later found that the company selling the home was trying to discourage them from purchasing the home. This family had gotten the house at a steal, far less than the going rate for the other homes being built in the neighborhood. Yes, God had stepped in again on their behalf. They continued to pray and told God that, when He blesses them with that house, they would honor Him by the way they cared for it.

It was finally time to close on their new home. Her credit was run one last time. Clean as a whistle. Good credit. Papers signed... keys given! What a glorious feeling. Who would have thought that, just months before, her credit was an embarrassment to say the least. To be holding those keys was truly a miracle.

While moving things into their marvelous new home, they noticed something peculiar, something that wasn't in the original floor plan of the house. "Is that flooring?" she asked. They asked the contractor foreman about it. He chuckled and said, "The workers mistakenly started adding flooring to what was supposed to be an open area upstairs, and I didn't stop them. I felt that, since you guys had so much difficulty during this process, you deserved extra square footage." The flooring provided them with additional square footage. Two additional rooms. Won't He Do It!?

Lesson to be learned:
Your circumstance is nothing for God.

Chapter 6

———∞———

Off the Charts

She had seen many years. Some would call her seasoned. She had always been in good health, strong and independent.

One day, she went for a doctor's visit and was told that her blood work revealed she was diabetic and that she has high blood pressure. They briefly educated her on what she should and should not eat. She listened and went home.

She continued to live life as if she was not diabetic. As if she didn't have high blood pressure. Weeks turned into months. Months turned into years. One pill became three. Three pills became five.

One morning, her daughter called her. She called daily but this day her daughter noticed that she didn't sound like herself. You see, she didn't just call her mom to check in. Most of their calls revolved around the goodness of God and how anything is possible through Him. During this call she sounded distant…confused. She just wasn't herself. Concerned, her daughter told her husband about the strange conversation she was having with her mom.

He immediately called the police and asked them to do a well check and gave them his wife's phone number.

The police called her back to inform her of what they found. Her mother was lying in bed. She had soiled the sheets, and they could see where she had attempted to eat. She was barely conscious. They told her daughter that they were taking her mom to the hospital and suggested that the daughter get to the hospital as soon as possible.

Her daughter began the 500-mile drive with her youngest son. As soon as they started, her phone rang. It was the doctor. He informed her that her mom's blood sugar was so high that it was off the charts for regular meters. They had to draw blood to get an accurate reading. The doctor said that he had never seen a number that high. To his amazement, she was not dead. She was not in a coma. Whenever they called her name, she was able to respond and then pass out.

The doctor asked her how long it would take her to arrive. The daughter told him that she was 500 miles away. With that, he told her that she probably was not going to make it, but whenever she arrived, no matter the time, the hospital would allow her up to the unit.

Shocked by the news she just received, she began weeping and praying, talking to God, telling Him, "Not today, Lord! Cover her, Father. Allow us to make it there in time." She felt that if she could just make it there. If she could just touch her mom, she would be alright.

Like most of us, our mothers mean the world to us. There's just something about mama. For her it was no different. The thought of losing her cut deep. It was almost too much to bear.

During the drive, her husband called to check in and became quickly aware of the extreme state she was in. He immediately told her to let their son drive. She objected to this because although their son had been learning to drive, he was not licensed. He had never driven a long distance. She also knew that with the state she was in, it would be best to turn over the car to her fifteen-year-old son. She instructed him, told him that it was a straight shot and that, when he got to their exit, she would take over. He did just that.

By the time they arrived at the hospital, it was night, well after visiting hours. She went to the front desk, and as promised, they allowed her entry.

As she reached the room, there her mom was lying in the fetal position. Even though she spoke with her mom on the phone daily, she had not seen her mom in months. This person lying there was not the memory she had of her mom. So frail, so helpless, but alive!

She touched her and thanked God. She then said, "Mom?!" With the most refreshing and sweetest sound, her mom responded by saying her daughter's name.

The doctor came in and stated that he had never seen anything like it. He was bewildered as to how she was still with us.

By morning, her numbers had improved. She was alert and talking. So much so that they decided that she was well enough to be moved to a regular hospital room.

While in that room, she became concerned with her appearance and what she was going to eat. Another great sign! There they were laughing, talking, doing hair and makeup. The hospital room had become a salon.

The next morning, the doctor informed them that she could be discharged.

From blood sugar readings so high it confused medical staff to being discharged from the hospital after two nights stay, God's work is truly amazing!

Lesson to be learned:
A diagnosis from man is not written in stone
when it comes to God.

Chapter 7

---∞---

The Lanai

When she lived in Hawaii, her condo was on the 23rd floor. This condo had a lanai with two chairs and a potted plant. The wind was so strong that the two patio chairs and the potted aloe plant would spend more time on their sides than upright. The aloe plant even started growing sideways.

She had always spent time with God in a room in past homes. With the condo having such limited space, she decided to dedicate the lanai as her prayer space and began meeting God at 4:00am daily on the lanai. With there being two chairs, she thought that she would sit in one and invite God to use the other. Even though people would visit her, she never let anyone sit in God's chair.

Once she started meeting God out there, she noticed something. The chairs had not moved. The plant stayed upright, and there were no insects. No matter how high the winds got, everything on the lanai stayed in place. This was strange seeing that, if she left a window in the living room open, which was right next to the lanai facing in the same direction, the decorations would be blown over.

She once came home from a difficult day at work. Things were also not going well at home. She went to her prayer lanai and put her head in her hands. She was heartbroken. Feeling lower than she had in a long time, she asked God that, with everything that she was doing in His name, why had He forgotten about her? She asked why should she continue? She felt like He had forsaken her. It was at that moment, that very moment, with tears streaming down her face, that the chair that had not moved since she started meeting Him out there, the one she had designated just for Him, started to shake. It shook so rigorously that it got her attention. As soon as she looked up, the chair stopped shaking. As if to say, "I hear you, and I'm with you." She knew that it was Him. She told Him that she heard Him and dried her tears. She began to pray about the desires of her heart and continued her daily routine with God.

A few months later, things drastically changed for the better. The things she prayed about, everything that was weighing heavily on her heart, it was resolved all at once. God had been listening...and He answered.

Lesson to be learned:
Even when we don't think so...God is listening.

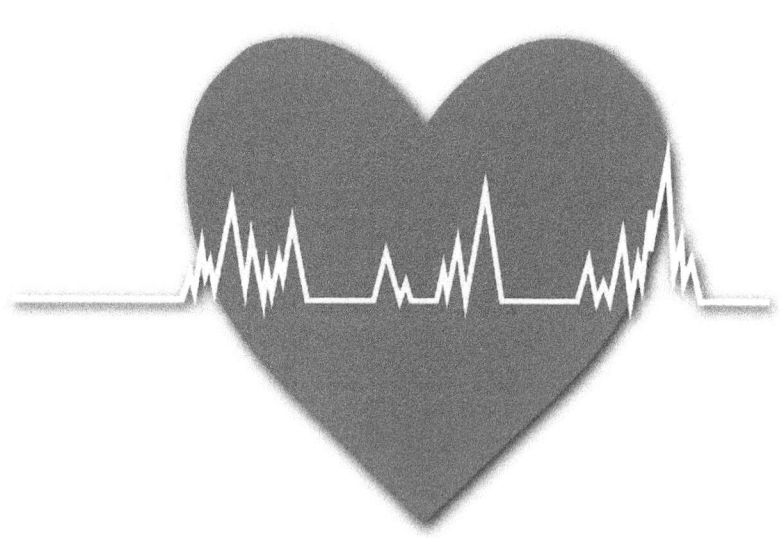

Chapter 8

———⚭———

The Heart Attack

Life had not been easy for this young man. He lived with his father. His father thought the world of him, and he loved his father deeply. And even though their bond was strong, that love could not pay the bills.

His father was not well. He had an extensive medical history. Because of his ailments, he wasn't able to work as he needed. He fell short and eventually their only option was to live in their car and move from place to place. Now, many would have let this circumstance destroy them but not this young man. He felt the love of his father, and that was enough for him.

He also had a love of sports. Sports were his outlet. His escape. Being on a team was everything. He became very good actually, one of the top players in the country. You see, when he played sports, the circumstances in his private life faded away. Even if it was just for a little while.

His father loved fishing, and on this day, his father asked him to go with him. Ordinarily, that would not have been an issue, but this was a school day, a day to see his friends and enjoy the sport he enjoyed so much. So on that day, he told his father he would rather go to school, and off he went.

After school, he waited on his father to pick him up like he always did, but this day was different; his cousin came. He was given the awful news. His father had collapsed on the pier and was rushed to the hospital. It was a heart attack. When he went to see his father, it did not look good. He prayed for his dad's recovery. He just wanted his dad to be better.

That night, he dreamed of his father. In this dream, his father came to him. He asked his father to take him with him, but his father told him that he couldn't but that he was going to be all right. When he awakened, sadness came over him. He knew that things would not be the same.

He later learned that his father died. Why was this happening? Not his dad! What was he to do? His dad was all that he had. What if this happened to him? He feared that he himself would one day have a heart attack.

He blamed God for his father's death. He began rebelling. He became a daredevil. He had no fear. He did things without worrying about the consequences. He had been told by many that he would never amount to anything, that he would die young. In his eyes, what was the point of going on?

As time went on, he had children. He loved them just as his dad loved him, but he never got over the hurt of losing his dad and all the negative predictions of naysayers. Over time, he matured a bit but still did not make the best decisions. Those decisions were weighing him down. One reason for this was because he could not get past the guilt of things from his past, the decisions that were holding him back in so many ways. He thought to himself, "How could God love me?"

He was dating someone. He had known her since childhood. She was the mother of his children. They met the year before his father died. She had tried over the years to get him to see how valuable his life truly was and that his children loved and needed him. There had been some people that would say to him that they saw God using him one day, that he had an anointing on his life. He always dismissed it.

He had a conversation with the mother of his girlfriend. He loved her as if she were his own mother. He had always seen good in her. She was a God-loving woman. Unlike others he had experienced in the church, he never saw her speaking of God and then acting like the world. So, he trusted what she would tell him. In that conversation, he told her about his hurts, the guilt he felt for the decisions he made over the years and how others would constantly remind him of what he did in his past, how there is no way to move on from the pain he's caused and the stupid decisions he has made. He told her how all of this was weighing him down. He said that she looked at him and told him that, if you ask God for forgiveness and truly mean it from your heart, He will forgive you. He died on the cross for our sins. Once you do, don't ever let anyone hold your past over you. Once God has forgiven you, you are washed clean. Don't look back. He felt this sense of relief and tried to live better.

Over time, even though he tried to leave his past behind, the stress of encountering problem after problem caught up with him. He woke up in the middle of the night. He had a pain in his chest that would not go away. The next day, he called his girlfriend and said to meet him at the hospital. When she got to the emergency room, he had already been taken back. They ran test after test. What he feared had occurred. "It's a heart attack.," they confirmed. All he could think of was that this is what his dad died of. His girlfriend started praying. She stayed with him the entire time he was in the hospital. She anointed his head with oil and continued to pray. After a couple of days, he was released from the hospital. He was instructed to follow up with his primary physician.

When he went home, he was weak and had lost his job due to the illness, but his girlfriend continued to pray and anoint him with oil until one day he just felt better. A complete turnaround. Like he had never been sick.

Eventually, he and his girlfriend went to his follow up appointment. While there, the doctor went over his medical record. The doctor discussed his hospital visit with them. He began to ask about the heart attack, to which the doctor replied, "There are no signs of a heart attack." "But they said that I had a heart attack at the hospital," he said. The doctor repeated, "There are no signs of a heart attack." They looked at each other as if to say, how could this be? They were relieved. He remembered the prayers, the anointing him with oil, and his conversation with a woman of God. He thought about all the things of his past, and yet God still showed mercy on him. He left there praising God's name.

He has since turned his life over to God, started making better decisions, working at a job he loves, and his relationship with his children has grown stronger. He was blessed with a new home and makes a point of honoring God by caring for his home as if God lives there, an act based on a promise he made to God while praying for a home. Right now, when something occurs, he'll beat you talking about how good God is and how, no matter what, God can fix it!

Lesson to be learned:
No matter how far you think you've gotten away from God…
He has never left you, nor has he stopped loving you.
God is just waiting on YOU.

Chapter 9

---∞---

The Dream Job

She had been on her job for a few years. She always entered new jobs wanting to do her best and to make things better than when she arrived. This job was no different.

At first, it seemed as though her work was appreciated. There was noticeable improvement in productivity. She was very proud of what God had allowed her to accomplish. They were also seeing profits for the first time in years, so much so that her boss and her boss's superior were getting bonuses and accolades.

Everything that seemed good soon took a turn for the worse. In time, all of the work was put on her. She would find her boss with their feet up shopping on the internet. When she asked for help, her boss would take offense to it. How dare she interrupt her. Who does she think she is asking for help?

She soon learned that her boss started plotting against her. On top of being responsible for all of the work, she was now scheduled to work six days a week and on call for seven. She started being micromanaged. She had to account for any space in her workday when she wasn't physically working. She also was written up for being insubordinate, an untruth that burned her to her core. When she met with her boss and her boss's superior, she found that she had been lied about. She soon realized that showing that she was upset just helped confirm the lie. She had no allies. At least that's how she felt.

She would get home filled with hurt and anger. She was consumed with how she was being treated. How could they? She didn't understand why these same people that were literally reaping the rewards of her hard work would now show themselves as her enemy.

She realized that being angry, letting it consume her once she got home, and complaining was not getting her anywhere. She asked for God to deliver her from the turmoil of this job. She prayed and told God that she was turning it over to him and began a twenty-one-day fast.

She returned to work, not bitter but with the feeling of being delivered from her situation. She refused to carry sadness or a sense of defeat. She had left the situation in God's hand.

A day came when she came across a job posting. It seemed like a dream. It was a dream location. The same place her mom had been saying for her entire life that she wanted to visit, the same one that in years past they had attempted to visit, but something would always happen and prevented them from going. She thought to herself, how cool would that be to live there?! It would make her mom's dream come true. She decided to apply. She felt that the worst that could happen is that they say no and go with someone else.

With each month that passed, she continued to do her best at work. She would approach each task, no matter how small, as if she was doing it for God. She actually noticed that she was smiling more. Her complaints had stopped.

After arriving home one evening, her phone rang. It was the job she had applied to so many months ago. After so much time she just assumed they had gone with someone else. The call went well. She felt like she had known the person on the other line forever. The interviewer told her that normally they would have her fly over for a face-to-face interview. This she worried about because it was an expensive trip. But then, they said something that stunned her. Because the job was so many miles away, they thought that they would do something a little different. They decided that, if she was interested, they would fly her over, put her in an apartment, and provide transportation for three months. Once she got there and both parties felt like this was a good fit, they would then extend it another three months to give her time to find a place to live and find her own transportation. That's a total of six months on the company's dime. That's six months of not having to worry about rent or transportation. If that were not enough, her pay would be almost double of what she was currently making.

When the call ended, she immediately began to praise God. Not only had he answered her prayer but through her, her mom's dream also became a reality. God...you've done it again!

Lesson to be learned:
With God...your enemies only think they have you down.

Chapter 10

———⚬———

Unobtainable

There was a vehicle. The vehicle of her dreams. From the moment she first saw it, she knew that it was THE CAR! Every time she saw someone driving down the road or saw one sitting on a car lot, she would imagine herself behind the wheel. This luxury vehicle had to be hers.

She would occasionally go to car dealerships just to get a closer look. The seats were like butter. The dashboard looked as though it had been plucked from her dreams. The exterior was sleek and refined. The price tag, in her present state, was unobtainable. Most would say impossible. It truly would be a miracle for her to be able to own one. That didn't stop her from praying for it. She didn't know how it was going to happen, but she believed that if she asked God for it that He would eventually bless her with one.

On a road trip with her boyfriend, she noticed her dream vehicle at a car lot on the other side of the highway. She pointed it out and her boyfriend said, "On the way back, we'll stop and look at it." He knew that if she saw one, like so many times in the past, they were going to have to stop. True to form, on the way back, they stopped at the car lot. It…was…beautiful! It was previously owned but in fantastic condition. It looked brand new. The interior was just as she imagined it. The exterior was as if the heavens had showered down the perfect hue. It sparkled!

After seeing them admiring the car, a gentleman approached. It was the owner of the dealership. "Can I help you guys?" They asked if they could get the keys and he agreed. She got behind the wheel and started the engine. A symphony. What a wonderful sound. They decided to take it for a test drive. The sheer joy on her face with every turn. It was a dream.

When they returned, the owner of the dealership stated that the vehicle was his mom's and that he agreed to sell it for her. He disclosed that his mom bought the vehicle, but then it became too expensive for her to maintain with the price of gas steadily rising, and due to his mom's age, she wanted to get rid of it.

She thought to herself, with how this vehicle looks and how it drives, there was no way she could afford it. Nothing new. She had been down this road before. Her boyfriend asked how much his mom was selling it for. The price that came out of his mouth was astounding. She thought, "With the money that I have and with some financing, I could probably handle that." But her boyfriend was not done. He pulled the owner aside. She didn't know what they were talking about, and at that moment she didn't care. She was close. Closer than she had ever been to owning her dream car.

When she looked up, they were both motioning for her to come to the office. She sat down, and what was said to her is what dreams are made of.

The gentleman stated that, when she gave him the money that she had, the vehicle would be hers. He then continued and revealed that her boyfriend had agreed to swap his car that they drove up in in exchange for her receiving her dream car.

No payments! An even swap! I don't think you understand the significance of that statement. Her dream car was an expensive car. The car being traded, although nice, was not expensive! Her down payment probably equated to a set of new tires for this vehicle. An even swap?! Really?!

Now before you say, "What was wrong with it"? NOTHING! Not one thing.

Her boyfriend stated that, to see her come so close to getting her dream vehicle, he had to make sure that it happened. The sweetest gift.

They unloaded everything that was in her boyfriend's car and placed them into her dream car and drove off the lot. She was driving her miracle that she now owned outright! It was all that she wanted and needed.

All she could think about was all the prayers that had gone up about the car, always saying, "I'm going to have that car," believing that someday God would provide it for her. She thanked God for this blessing.

She prayed over that car, took care of that car, and it took care of her. Over the years, she had no major problems with it. Eventually, though she loved this car, it was time to move on to the next vehicle. Her boyfriend made some repairs to it, and the vehicle was traded in on another vehicle.

Some time passed, and her boyfriend called her to tell her what he had just witnessed. He was at a gas station when all of a sudden, the "dream car" pulled in. He said that a young mother and her kids were in it. He said that he told the lady that his girlfriend was the previous owner and wanted to assure her that it was a reliable car. He said that she was grateful to hear that because she had had so many issues in the past. It was nice to know that the vehicle she once loved, and still holds a place in her heart for, was now being a blessing to someone else.

To this day, how God blessed her with her dream car blows her mind.

Lesson to be learned:
Trust and believe. There is nothing unobtainable for God.

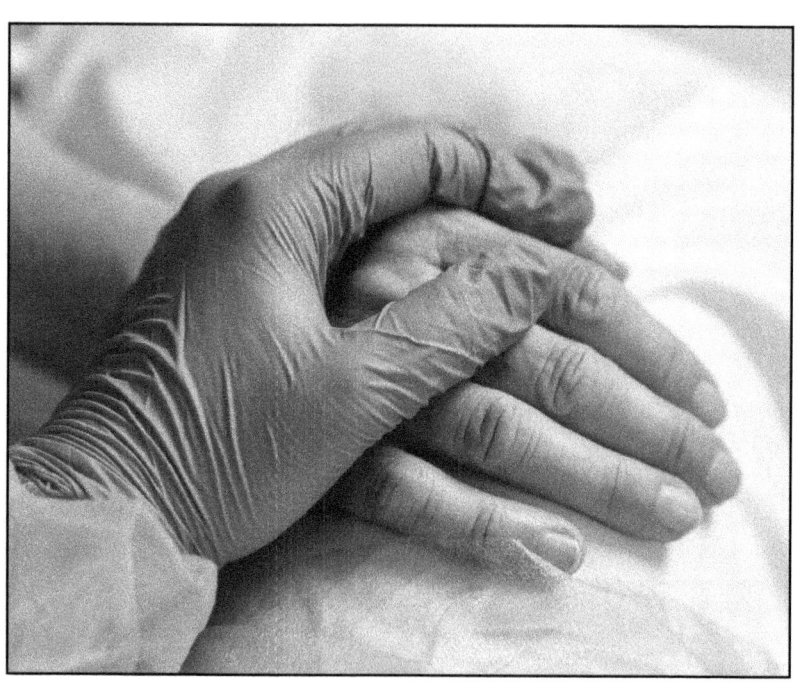

Chapter 11

───────⊸⊷⊷───────

The Delay

She had a job that she hated. I know, I know that "hated" is a strong word, but she could not think of a more accurate word to describe her disdain for this job. It was an interesting situation. On one hand, she knew that God led her there. On the other hand, how can this place that God led her to come with all of the problems and have her develop a true hate for it? She began looking for another job to no avail.

She would get up in the morning and not want to get out of bed because she knew where she was headed. When she got there, she would sit in the car and say to the Lord, "I know you've got something better for me." She knew that she would be treated poorly once inside. But knowing who her Heavenly Father was, she would put a smile on her face and count down the hours until it was time to go home. She would talk to God, sometimes out of anger and frustration. She would ask, "Why am I here? Why would you have me going through all of this? Why would you place me here?" And with the clarity of hearing a pin drop in a silent room, she heard, "It's not the job. It's what I need you to learn from it and what I need you to do." From that point on, she decided to make the most of the situation. She started asking each day before walking into the building, "What would You have me to do today, Lord?" She'd put a smile on her face and begin her day.

There was a day when she was working with a coworker. They both had a patient that, for whatever reason, they couldn't get to in their first attempt. Because of the location of these patients, they decided to trade. They then continued to attend to the patients they now had on their respective lists.

When she got to this one room, the patient was lying in bed. She introduced herself and proceeded to begin the exam. During the exam, the patient started talking about his ailments. He also stated that, with all of his health problems, he was thinking about turning his life over to God. He also said that he was thinking of doing it the Sunday coming, but he was in the hospital and wouldn't be able to do it. She looked at him and told him that if he wanted to turn his life over to God, he didn't have to wait. They could do it right then. "Really?" he said in astonishment. "Sure," she said. "All you have to do is say, Lord Jesus, You are the Savior of my soul. I believe with all my heart that God raised You from the dead, and with my mouth, I now confess You as the Lord of my life. I believe all my sins are washed away in Your precious blood, and I receive the gift of eternal life and the gift of Your righteousness. In Jesus' mighty name. Amen." He exclaimed, "That's it? Thank You!" She instructed him to go to church with his wife once he got out of the hospital. She gave him some scriptures to read and wished him well.

When she left the room, she had a smile on her face. She realized why she was there. According to his Word, God had left the ninety-nine and gone after the one. She said to herself, "I'll get a new job now." Within a week, she received notification of a job that was open at another facility. She applied and got the job. She would be working better hours, which meant free time and less stress. A perfect fit. Something she had been praying for.

Lesson to be learned:

Sometimes what you're going through isn't about you. Sometimes God is lining you up for a task that, if completed, will lead you to greater.

Chapter 12

———∞———

Perseverance

She was young, nine months pregnant, and in labor but not your typical labor. She noticed that she had not had one major pain. A little discomfort early on but nothing since. Hours had passed until...

She was lying there watching television when a sharp pain hit her. The pain was so intense that it took her breath away. It was as if all the labor pains had rolled up into one. She could not speak, not even to call her mom who was in the same room with her. She lay there so long that her mother had fallen asleep. The only way to let her mom know that it was time to go to the hospital was to bang against the wall. Her mother arose, and she told her that it was time.

As she stood, she realized that maybe it wasn't such a good idea to have sat there as long as she had. Upon self-examination, she became aware that this guy was closer to meeting the world than she was previously aware. She thought to herself, "Do I call an ambulance or continue to the hospital as planned?" She chose the latter. While walking to the car, all she could think was, "Hang on there, little buddy. Don't exit now! That would not be pretty."

While she sat reclined in the passenger seat of the vehicle, she could see the stars. The sky was so clear that night. Then, in the blink of an eye, she felt pressure, the child went airborne from her womb, and she caught him mid-flight. Instant mom-of-the-year nomination behavior if you ask me, but let us continue.

He didn't let out a cry. He just looked up at her as if in amazement with the look of, "So this is what you look like." He let out a little cough to which her mom almost wrecked the car because when they left the house there were two of them, and now there were three. It was dark, so her mom didn't see the unbelievable catch that occurred earlier.

As they approached the hospital. Her mom, in hysterics by this point, got out of the car and told a nurse standing outside the situation. A handful of people came running out with a stretcher. When they looked, they became concerned. When the child made his debut, the cord was wrapped around his neck. Because of this, he was not getting enough oxygen. They stated that her cradling him in her lap instead of lifting him to her chest was a blessing. She would have cut off his air supply entirely.

Some years went by. He was an incredibly happy and joyful little boy. But soon she began noticing that he was not talking like other kids his age. Mostly gibberish. She also noticed that his behavior was not sufficient for his age. She talked to the day care staff, and they were also concerned. He was to start school soon. She wondered what would be best for him. The staff recommended that he be held back from starting school on time, that it would be ideal if he stayed back a year and started school with his younger brother. She was also told by many that she would probably have to care for him most of his life, that he would never be independent.

As a parent, this was a hard pill to swallow. This was her son. You just don't want your child to suffer due to limitations.

However, she ultimately agreed. She did feel that no matter what, if this was the card they were dealt, she would make the most of it. She decided that she would pray over him. She asked God to surround her son with people that would help him to become the person God created him to be. To cover him. She then let go and let God.

He eventually started talking, and once he started school, he was constantly picked on and teased. When given an assignment in reading, he would always have to read a book twice in order to comprehend what was written. When there was a test coming, he would study and study to make sure he would pass. In contrast, his brother would not study and would ace the test. To watch him was truly remarkable. There he was. This little boy. He dealt with obstacle after obstacle, but it never stopped him. He would just put a smile on and try harder.

He began carrying a Bible. When she opened it, it was filled with color-coded highlighted passages along with tabs. It made her admire his struggle the more.

Eventually, he grew, went off to college, had leading roles in plays, obtained a job, and began living on his own. This young man who started off with what some would call a bleak future was now independent and doing well. So well, in fact, that the people on his job loved him. He started getting recognition at work followed by promotions and even better jobs with more responsibilities.

She thought back on all the negative things that had been said and all the things that had been done to her child. With that came a sense of pride and gratefulness to God. She also felt admiration for his perseverance and what he had accomplished in the face of adversary.

She reflected on her first meeting with him, cradled in her arm, and she said to herself, "Maybe, when he looked up at me for the first time, it was not to say, 'So this is what you look like.' Maybe he was saying, "Don't worry, Mom, sit back and see what God and I will do!"

Lesson to be learned:
When people try to dictate who you are or what you will be, ask yourself, "Is that what God said?"

Chapter 13

———∞———

The Sheriff

This was a simpler time. A time when two brothers resided in the South. The older one, even though there were no favorites, was a mother's dream: always obedient, always helping whenever he could. He had become a husband and a father. A protector. A generous soul. His younger brother, however…Let's just say that he was a challenge. A loveable mischief. A good person, but if there was a choice between smooth sailing and rough seas, he was going to choose rough seas every time. It was just the way that he was.

One evening, the younger brother went to a bar like he had done many times before. While there, he began to talk loudly. An annoyance is what he was. At this point, one of the patrons left the bar and went to the older brother's house. When he got there, he told him that he needed to go to the bar and get his brother, so they both headed back to the bar. When the older brother got to the bar, the situation had escalated. Apparently, two other men decided that they had had enough of the younger brother's antics. They had begun fighting the younger brother. When the older brother saw that it was two against one, he ran in to help his brother. Not liking the new odds, one of the other men pulled out a gun. A struggle ensued, and the gun went off. Silence fell over the room. Was anyone hurt? One of the other men fell to the floor. Life had left him. The police were called, and the two brothers were taken to jail.

Eventually, the news got back to their mother. Her relationship with God was strong. She began praying for the family of the other man and asking God to cover her boys. She later found that there was talk of the two of them being put to death for what had occurred. The mother asked God for guidance. Even though they were adults, they were still her children. I don't care how old they get; they are always your babies.

While praying, she heard it clearly. She was instructed to go to the sheriff's house. This was unheard of. She began speaking to God. "Go to the sheriff's house? Lord, no one does this. By the time I get there, it will be supper time." Again, she heard, "Go to the sheriff's house." And with that, she began walking.

When people saw her, they asked where she was going. She told them that she was going to the sheriff's house. Those that asked became fearful for her. Fearful of what would happen to her, showing up at the sheriff's house. Who did this black woman think she was walking up to the sheriff's house? To make matters worse, it was supper time. No one interrupts the sheriff at supper time.

When she got to the house, she took one step on the porch and said, "Lord, Lord" and knocked on the door. The sheriff's wife answered, "May I help you?" "Yes. I'd like to speak with the sheriff," she stated. The wife said, "Well, he just sat down for supper and..." She was interrupted by the sheriff exclaiming, "Who is that?!" His wife told him. To their amazement, they heard footsteps approaching. The sheriff had come to the door. "What's going on?" he asked. "I need your help," the mother said. "It's my boys. They were arrested for murder." And without batting an eye, he grabbed his hat. His wife said, "But what about your food?" "I'll eat it when I return," he said. They both went to the jail.

When they got there, the sheriff walked in. This presence. This force of nature. He says, "You've got two boys back there accused of murder?" "Yes sir," the officers said. "Let 'em out!" the sheriff said. Bewildered, they asked, "Pardon me, sir?" The sheriff said, "I said, let them out! Drop the charges and let them out!" They got the key and unlocked the cell. The brothers walked out to their mother's embrace. With the room still in shock as to what had just occurred, the mother began to thank the sheriff. The sheriff nodded, put his hat back on, and left the building.

Lesson to be learned:
When you think that there is no way out, God can
use the most unlikely sources to be your saving grace.

Chapter 14

———∞———

The Eleventh Hour

She had gone to school and begun a career, a career she was grateful to have. This job meant security, a leg up for her family. Up to this point, life was a struggle, but with this new job, she would be bringing home far more money than she had in the past.

She absolutely loved her job and was extremely good at it. During a company meeting, the boss stated that there was an account, the company's largest account, that they were on the verge of losing. The reason was that they just weren't seeing the returns they were hoping for. The boss stated that she needed them to think of a way to increase revenue in hopes that they would remain a client.

She got to work. She researched and researched ways to bring in more money for the client. Studied the ins and outs of their account and realized that there were ways to bring in more money that they had been overlooking for years. She brought this up to her boss's attention and, with her approval, began implementing the new strategy.

First month, a noticeable increase. Second month, even more. The client was impressed. Eventually, she was solely responsible for this client's account, so much so that the client started calling her directly with any questions they had. They soon requested that she come to the meetings at their facility with her boss.

During this time, she thought to herself that she should become certified. She asked to meet with her boss to tell her her plan. During the meeting, her boss stated that her daughter was already going to class to be certified and that she would send her to the same class that her daughter was attending.

When she got to class, she realized that what her boss told her was not true. The boss's daughter had not already been in classes. Her daughter was signing up for classes at the same time she was. She realized that the boss did not want her to have any advantage within the company. Because she loved what she did, she went to classes and continued increasing revenue for the client. She was given another account and then another. She handled them with ease.

One day, the client called her and asked if she would be interested in coming to work for them directly. Even though that sounded great and she could probably ask for whatever she wanted and get it, she turned it down because she had signed a non-compete agreement when she was hired. She could not work for any client of the company she was currently working for.

While working, a co-worker, an absolute angel, asked her what her long-term plans were. She stopped and realized that she had never thought about that before. You see, this job that she loved had her making more money than she had ever made before. Honestly, she thought that she had arrived…reached the ultimate goal. The co-worker told her, "You have kids, and this job has a salary cap and no benefits. Once you reach that cap, there will be no more raises. You'll be stuck! Why don't you go back to school and get a degree in a field where there is growth?

I would, but I'm not getting any younger, and at this point, I'm just waiting on retirement. Think of your future." Initially, she dismissed the advice, but it was playing on repeat in the back of her mind.

Another company meeting was called. The boss had an announcement. The boss's daughter would be coming in to learn the ropes. She would be starting from the bottom and working her way up. They were asked to help her learn the business. Nonetheless, when her daughter arrived, she was introduced as their new boss. Everyone looked around the room at each other as if to say, "You have got to be kidding me." So there they were, graced with the task of training their new boss. The very same person that didn't pass her certification course was now their boss. At that point, her mind flashed back to her conversation with her co-worker. That very same night, she went home and began looking up schools that she could apply to. She decided that she needed to continue to work, so she would have to take a course that was offered at night, but every course that she looked at only had classes offered during the day. A few days later, she received a postcard in the mail that said, "We've been trying to reach you. Give us a call at…." Curiosity got the best of her, so she called the phone number listed. The voice on the other end was very pleasant. It was a recruiter at a technical college. The conversation went well, and an appointment was made to go to the school. When she arrived, she didn't know what to expect. She still didn't know what course she wanted to take. The recruiter told her that she needed to take an assessment test to see what course would be best for her. According to the scores obtained, she was told that she qualified for the cardiac program. She had never heard of this particular type of cardiac program, so the recruiter recommended that they tour a class that was in session. Looking at all of the equipment, she was in awe at the fact that she could one day be doing this as a career. She then learned that the course was offered at night. She could work during the day and go to school at night. It was exactly what she needed, so she decided to join the program.

With work by day, school by night and children at home, it was a lot to take on, but she was doing it. She began thinking outside of the box. She even became one of the top students in her class. She did not tell anyone at work except for that one coworker. As time went on, she grew closer and closer to the internship for school. One of her instructors approached her and stated that he wanted to place her at his facility to work with him during her externship but realized that his facility was too far of a drive, so he decided to place her with the next best thing. She was placed at a facility that was known nationally and close to home. Everything was great! The problem was that her internship had to be performed during the day. That meant no pay for six months. How would she be able to do this? Her job was during the day, and there was no night shift. She needed the money. She had kids…responsibilities. She prayed about it. She said, "Lord, how can I go six months without pay? I need you to step in on my behalf and make a way."

So the time had finally arrived. That Sunday, she had decided that she would put in her letter of resignation on that coming Friday and just see what God would do to cover her expenses. Monday morning, she went to work and started her day as usual. Near the end of the day, her boss called her to the office. She sat there wondering what this was about. Her boss said to her that she was going to have to let her go. This brought a smile to her face. Ordinarily, this would be a sad time for most, but because she was fired, that meant unemployment benefits. Benefits that would bring in money to her household for, you guessed it… six months. With this news, she began thanking God, which confused her boss. She walked out of that company with a broad smile on her face and her eyes fixed on her future. There was no looking back. In the eleventh hour, God had delivered!

She finished her internship and received her first job in her new career. She couldn't believe that she thought that she had arrived with the pay on that last job. This job was challenging and paid her an amount that made it possible to move into better, drive better, and provide a life for her kids that would make them better.

When she got settled, she called the angel that God had placed at her old job. Her now "former" co-worker. She thanked her. Thanked her for prompting her to think beyond the here and now. For cheering her on with each passing grade. For seeing a future in her that she didn't see for herself. The one who reminded her whose child she was.

With this experience, it occurred to her that she was thinking too small. That God had bigger and better for her. She has since gone on to help countless others realize their dreams. She has even started businesses that help and assist others. She is walking the path that God has placed before her.

Lesson to be learned:
When you've gone as far as you think you can go and have reached the edge of this thing called life, take another step and watch God elevate you.

Chapter 15

———∞———

One Day

When they were young, just kids really, they dreamed of having more in life. It seemed unlikely given their current situation. You see, they had challenges financially. Well, that's an understatement. I think the correct description would be: They were poor. That's a more accurate description. They were poor, but they found opportunity and hope in everything. They never saw themselves that way.

She remembers fondly that on their first date, they went to a burger joint. He ordered two large burgers, a large order of fries, and a large drink. He then turned to her and said, "What do you want?" That is the appetite she would come to know all too well over the years. After she ordered her food, they sat and talked about their dreams and what they wanted for their futures. Their eyes would light up when they talked about houses, cars, and what they wanted their bank accounts to look like. They talked about family and friends. By the end of the evening, they both knew that the other was a keeper.

They started working at an early age. Extra shifts and second jobs were the norm to make ends meet. However, there was no question for either of them that they would one day be successful.

When they got home from work, they would talk about their day and, as a treat, scrape together the little change they had and go to a late-night restaurant and order off the dollar menu. As they returned home, they would sit on the hood of the car looking up at the stars. The stars seemed so bright, so close. They would imagine themselves going on trips, living in beautiful homes, and driving nice cars. They would often say, "One day, we're going to live like that."

It was common for them to drive through nice neighborhoods and imagine themselves living there. They would look at the yards and say, "That's what we should put in our yard." As if they already had a yard.

They would go to car dealerships and test drive expensive cars (expensive for them) and imagine owning one. There were many times when they would be driving their own car and pull up next to an expensive car at the traffic light, and with a smile, they would say, "One day we're going to drive a car that nice."

They would go to open houses and walk through those homes in amazement, taking a mental note of what they loved about those homes so that when God blessed them with their own home, they could purchase those same items.

While looking through a newspaper, she saw the floor plan of a home that she could see herself living in. She clipped it out and put it in her wallet. She would look at it often and say, "One day, this will be our home." She looked at the clipping so much that it became worn at the folds and around the edges.

Over the years, they had horrible cars that they had to share. So horrible that, if you looked at them the wrong way, they would break down. But that didn't stop him from going outside, washing it, and detailing it as if it were the most expensive car in the world. He would always say that God blessed him with it, so he was going to take care of it.

They also rented many homes over the years. Each time they would take care of it as if it were their own. So much so that they often left it in better condition than when they first moved in. Others would say to them, "Why are you investing your money in someone else's property? You're not going to get that money back. That's crazy!" To which they would always reply, "If we take care of this home as if it were ours, one day God will bless us with our own."

The years passed. Better jobs were obtained, which came with better pay. They were able to purchase a home and then another. They also acquired condominiums. Their home filled with all the things they dreamed it would. Over time, their driveway filled with two cars, then three, then four. It took a lot of time, struggle, and determination, but suddenly life was good.

One day while driving, they stopped at a traffic light. They noticed movement coming from the car next to them. When they looked, there was a young man asking them to roll down their window. When they did, he leaned out his window and with admiration he said, "I really like your car. It's really nice!" They thanked him. In that very moment, they looked at each other and realized that they had reached their "One Day."

She suggested that they go out to dinner. But not just any dinner. She thought that they should pay homage to those two young kids. Their younger selves. Those two kids that would gaze at the stars and dream. Those same kids that faced so many challenges. Those same kids that knew about God's grace and favor.

At that dinner, they thanked God for all he had blessed them with. They also thanked their younger selves for not making excuses and not giving up. For believing that they indeed would reach their one day.

Lesson to be learned:
Words have power. Your attitude is powerful. Think before you speak. Your future depends on it. The words you speak today are the foundation for your tomorrow.

Chapter 16

————∞————

The Homegoing

Her mom lived with her and her husband. Over the years there had been many health scares concerning her mom. So much so that she used to joke and say that, when her mom dies, it would be something that has nothing to do with previous hospital visit ailments.

Thanksgiving, Christmas, and yet another birthday came and went for her mom. If we're being accurate, she actually celebrated her eightieth birthday twice because her oldest grandson got the years mixed up. She was spoiled both times. Good times! Having her in their lives was truly a blessing.

Her mom had lived to see eighty-one years, and even though in the last few she developed signs of dementia and wasn't able to do all the things she used to do with ease, she still had her humor.

One day, her mom was at home with her husband. For many years they had endless conversations and laughs. During this talk, something was said that scared her son-in-law. He said that she looked at him and said two simple words, "I'm tired." What scared him about those words was the way she said it. As if to say she was tired of the ailments, tired of the lack of independence, tired of having to be cared for, tired of just existing, not living.

She would check in on her mom every morning to make sure she had everything she would need for the day, but this particular morning, there was no response. She was breathing—but no response. She tried to waken her. Nothing. She tried again. Little movement. At this point she thought, "Her blood sugar must have dropped during the night. I've got to get her to ingest something sweet." This had happened in the past, so she knew exactly what to do. She made sugar water and put the rim of the cup to her mom's mouth. One sip down...two sips down. "Good, she'll be back in no time," she thought. Three sips, four sips, five sips....She's still not back. She's usually back to herself by now. The decision was made to call an ambulance.

She contacted the kids and her husband to let them know that Grandma had been taken to the hospital. She had five children who were all adults at this point. Her four sons treated their grandmother like the queen that she was. They loved on her, and Grandma wanted for nothing. Her only daughter, who was always said to be so much like Grandma, over the years would be told, "You see your grandma? That's you in fifty years." They would all laugh because of how accurate that statement was. So much alike.

The kids came to visit Grandma in the hospital. And even though she had been in and out of hospitals over the years and always bounced back, somehow they all knew this time was different. They brought in the New Year with her in the hospital. Where did she go? Yes, that was her body lying in the bed, but where's that fire, that spark, that bounce back? The doctor informed her that they recommended placing Grandma on hospice at home. So they did.

She arrived home via ambulance. There in the corner of her room was the chair that she adored. Still there, but now there's something new. A hospital bed front and center with all the items around it necessary to care for her.

From sunrise to sunset, Grandma was cared for. She was just happy to have her mom home. It didn't matter what the circumstances were. She just wanted her home.

Suddenly, while doing ordinary tasks around the house, God spoke to her regarding her mom. He let her know that soon her mom would be leaving her. She asked, "When?" It would be in two months. Around her birthday, in fact. This crushed her. For one, even though she expected to outlive her mom, it still was horrible to think about. And two, near her birthday? Forever after, she would remember the passing of her mom around the same time as celebrating her own birthday. But at that moment, none of that mattered. She now knew that it wasn't a matter of if. It was when.

She then began to contact everyone, without letting them know what she had been told, to insist that they meet one last time while Grandma was still with them. She wanted a family photo and for everyone to love on Grandma, gathered in the same place, one last time. They all met at a restaurant. They laughed, they loved; it was family! Secretly, they all felt that this was the last time they would all be together with her, even though no one could bring themselves to utter those words aloud.

Once they all parted, she drove home with her husband in the passenger seat and Grandma lying in the back seat. On the ride home, she looked in the back seat, and there Grandma was, sitting straight up. Almost looking over their shoulders. It scared them and made them both laugh all at the same time. You see, on the way to the restaurant, she lay almost in the fetal position the entire ride. But after seeing everyone, it was as if she had new life! It was good to see. When they got home and put Grandma to bed, she and her husband thought fondly of the time they spent with the family.

As time went on, Grandma grew weaker and weaker, slowly leaving behind fragments of what she used to be. The conversations they once shared were long gone. She sat in Grandma's favorite chair right next to her and said, "Mom, I just want you to know that I love you, and I am so blessed that God gave you to me as my mom. You did a good job." Without hesitation, Grandma turned to her and said, "Thank you, I tried real hard." She was floored and honored. To be able to tell Grandma what her heart was feeling and that God allowed Grandma to actually respond was truly a miracle in itself. A precious moment. A moment she carries with her always.

With a heavy heart, all she could think of was that her birthday was soon approaching. Not much longer now.

One night, Grandma had a seizure. This was new. With all the things Grandma dealt with in the past, there was never a seizure. All she could do was hold Grandma's hand, comfort her by telling her that she was with her, and wait it out.

The next morning, she got up like she normally did, made sure Grandma and the hospice aides had what they were going to need for the day. While she was in Grandma's room, there it was again. Another seizure. Again, she held Grandma's hand, but this time hit her differently. To see her that way. She remembered what God had said. It was exactly two weeks from her birthday. With a tear streaming down her face, she turned her head away and prayed silently, "Lord, she has been a good and faithful servant. She doesn't deserve this. Please do not let her suffer like this." At that moment, it stopped. The seizure stopped. You see, Grandma had been a praying woman. A woman that read her Bible hours at a time. She spoke about God's goodness to whomever would listen, had taken care of many, and asked little. A truly good woman.

She continued getting ready to leave for work, but as she always did, she looked in on Grandma and said, "I'm getting ready to go. I love you!" All of a sudden, Grandma lifted her head as if to say something. Something Grandma had not done in weeks. She waited, but nothing came out. So again, she said, "Ok, I love you!" and proceeded to leave.

She went about her morning at work as she always had. A few hours later, her husband called her. "You need to come home," is all he said. She, as if in denial, said, "Why? What's going on?" To which he repeated, "You need to come home." Immediately, tears streamed from her eyes. She knew. Grandma was gone. Just when God said she would be.

On the way home, she cried, praised God, and thanked Him for allowing this woman, this wonderful woman, to be her mom. She thought back on the countless conversations, the praise encounters at home, the impromptu dances with her mom in her room as a child, and of course, the laughs. Oh, how they laughed!

When she pulled up in front of the house, she got out of the car. The nurse was sitting on the porch. Her husband stood, her rock, her shoulder to cry on, and that is exactly what she did. She fell into his arms and wept. Moments later, it was time to stand at the throne and salute the Queen! She looked so peaceful. As if she was just sleeping. She stood over her and told her once again how much she loved and appreciated her. "What a ride, Old Lady!" as she fondly used to call Grandma. "You can rest now. I love you!"

Everyone that called to give their condolences had one thing in common. They all commented on Grandma's laughter. How infectious it was. Her grandkids made a point of doing and saying things just to hear it. Thank God for technology. They can still hear Grandma's voice even though she's gone.

The day of Grandma's funeral, the immediate family gathered. The mood, understandably, was somber. Some could not bring themselves to enter the sanctuary until the funeral started. They all sat in solidarity. Each just wanting it to end. Not wanting to see the Queen in this state.

Once the service was over, they all went graveside to say one last goodbye. One of her grandsons stood to speak of kind and wonderful memories of his grandma. It was so touching and heartfelt. He then took his seat. Tears started to flow within the group, some on the verge of breaking down. Another grandson, who was very animated, stood to speak and shared a special memory of a time with Grandma. He began by talking about one occasion when Grandma stayed with him. She was sitting in a robe on the side of the bed. He brought her a salad to eat with her favorite salad dressing. She loved French dressing. He said that he went downstairs to get her something to drink. When he returned, his eyes widened, jaw dropped. There Grandma was, sitting with one boob in the salad covered in dressing and the other boob tucked under her armpit. As soon as those words left his lips, Grandma's granddaughter, the one that had always been told that she was just like Grandma, erupted into this from-the-gut laughter. So much so that she fell over into the next chair from laughing so hard. Everyone, including the funeral staff, began hysterically laughing. It was as if Grandma was there laughing through her granddaughter. It's exactly what everyone needed. As far as they all were concerned, the funeral was over.

As they all gathered at the house, she looked around, and with warmth in her heart, she closed her eyes and smiled. Laughter and more laughter filled her home. Grandma would be so proud!

She thought about what God had told her leading up to this moment, and with gratitude...she thanked Him.

Lesson to be learned:
Many people don't get the opportunity to tell their loved ones how they feel about them before they pass on. No matter the situation, whatever you want to say to a loved one that's still with us…consider this your invitation to do so. You'll never get that time back once they're gone.

IN LOVING MEMORY OF DOROTHY...A.K.A G-MA

Thank you, Mom, for being the best Mutré, Granny,
and G-ma there ever was!

I will forever cherish our countless conversations about God's
goodness over the years. Know that they have touched
and will continue to reach generations to come.
In honor of you...Rest well, Old Lady! We love and miss you.

Biography

Adrian Read is a Christian author with a heart for sharing the transformative power of faith through storytelling. Inspired by the real-life testimonies of grandmas and loved ones as well as their own spiritual journey, Adrian writes to encourage, uplift, and strengthen believers in their walk with God. Adrian combines biblical truths with relatable life experiences, creating narratives that resonate with readers seeking hope, purpose, and a deeper relationship with Christ. Adrian's debut book, *From Acts to Testimonies*, is a testament to her passion for spreading God's love and wisdom, offering insight and inspiration for those navigating life's challenges with faith.

www.ingramcontent.com/pod-product-compliance
Ingram Content Group UK Ltd.
Pitfield, Milton Keynes, MK11 3LW, UK
UKHW021352191225
9677UKWH00051B/1003